How to Talk to Anyone as an Introvert

The 5 Steps Path from Awkwardness to Charisma by Becoming a Small Talk Master Who Wins Friends and Builds Meaningful and True Connections

Ethan Blaze

© **Copyright 2023 Ethan Blaze - All rights reserved.**

This document is geared towards providing exact and reliable information in regard to the topic and issue covered.

- From a Declaration of Principles which was accepted and approved equally by a Committee of the American Bar Association and a Committee of Publishers and Associations.

In no way is it legal to reproduce, duplicate, or transmit any part of this document in either electronic means or in printed format. All rights reserved.

The information provided herein is stated to be truthful and consistent, in that any liability, in terms of inattention or otherwise, by any usage or abuse of any policies, processes, or directions contained within is the solitary and utter responsibility of the recipient reader. Under no circumstances will any legal responsibility or blame be held against the publisher for any reparation, damages, or monetary loss due to the information herein, either directly or indirectly.

Respective authors own all copyrights not held by the publisher.

The information herein is offered for informational purposes solely and is universal as so. The presentation of the information is without contract or any type of guarantee assurance.

The trademarks that are used are without any consent, and the publication of the trademark is without permission or backing by the trademark owner. All trademarks and brands within this book are for clarifying purposes only and are owned by the owners themselves, not affiliated with this document.

Table of contents

INTRODUCTION 7

CHAPTER 1: THE RIGHT MINDSET, A NEW FRAMEWORK FOR THINKING ABOUT YOURSELF 12
- AS YOU FEEL INSIDE, YOU PROJECT OUTSIDE 12
- IF YOU BELIEVE IT, YOU BELIEVE IT 14
- DISEMPOWERING PHRASES THAT LIMIT 15
- CHARACTERISTICS OF SOMEONE AFRAID TO SOCIALIZE 16
  - *Why Does It Appear?* 17
  - *Is Shyness a Social Phobia?* 17
- REFRAMING INSECURE THOUGHTS 19
- INTROSPECT AT THE ORIGIN OF INSECURITIES 20
  - *Relationship with Parents* 20
  - *Social Anxiety* 20
  - *Recent Failures* 21
  - *Perfectionism* 21
- CHALLENGE NEGATIVE THOUGHTS 21
  - *Record Bad Thoughts* 21
  - *Ask Yourself Questions* 22
  - *Be Realistic* 22
  - *Look for Different Perspectives* 22
  - *Embrace the Uncomfortable* 23
  - *Accept Errors* 23
  - *Don't Push Yourself So Hard* 23
  - *Broaden the Picture* 24
  - *Don't Compare Yourself* 24
  - *Try* 24
  - *List Your Strengths and Qualities* 24
- TECHNIQUES FOR APPROACHING CONVERSATIONS IF YOU'RE SHY ... 26
  - *Acknowledge Your Shyness* 26
  - *Make a Compliment* 26
  - *Appeal to the Classic* 26
  - *Smile and Make Eye Contact* 27
  - *Answer with Questions* 27
  - *Respect Each Other's Space* 27
  - *Dose Personal Information* 28
  - *Listen Before You Speak* 28
  - *Avoid Controversial Topics* 28
  - *Don't Lie* 29
- LEARN HOW TO OVERCOME SHYNESS WITH THESE STEPS 29

Speak Without Fear of Insecurity, Do Not Put Masks or Hide It 29
Go Back to Thoughts That Cause You Insecurity 30
Work Healthy Selfishness 30
Express Your Thoughts and Feelings 30
Value Yourself, Love Yourself, Take Care of Yourself 31
Learn to Say No and Make Decisions Based on It 31
Don't Compare Yourself to Others 31
Act As If 32
Dare for New Things 32

CHAPTER 2: INTROVERSION AS THE STRONGEST CONVERSATIONAL WEAPON 34

EXTROVERTS HAVE A REPUTATION FOR BEING GOOD LEADERS 34
DOES INTROVERSION EQUAL SHYNESS? 35
CHARACTERISTICS OF INTROVERTS 35
AS AN INTROVERT, THERE IS A LOT YOU CAN GIVE 37
YOU CAN BE A GREAT LEADER 37
WHY IS THIS HAPPENING? 38
AS AN INTROVERT, YOU CAN PRACTICE ACTIVE LISTENING AND MINDFUL OBSERVATION 38
ACTIVE LISTENING TECHNIQUES 39
ACTIVE LISTENING DYNAMICS 40
ACTIVE LISTENING EXERCISES 43
View a Conversation 43
The Bus 44
The Blind Man 45
Selective Listening 45
Tell Me Your Story 47
Observe the Other Person's Appearance 48

CHAPTER 3: BODY LANGUAGE AS YOUR BUSINESS CARD 49

THE IMPACT OF NONVERBAL LANGUAGE ON VERBAL LANGUAGE 50
TYPES OF NONVERBAL COMMUNICATION 51
Expressions on the Face 51
Gestures 51
Paralinguistics 52
Posture and Body Language 53
Proxemics 53
Look with Your Eyes 53
Appearance 54
SOFTEN TECHNIQUE AND NON-VERBAL COMMUNICATION 54
WHAT DOES THE SOFTEN TECHNIQUE OF NONVERBAL COMMUNICATION MEAN? 55

WHAT IS THE F1 SCORE IN THE SOFTEN TECHNIQUE? 56
WHAT IS THE SOFTEN TECHNIQUE? 57
   S: Smile 57
   O: Open Posture 57
   F: Leaning Forward 58
   T: Take Notes 58
   E: Eye Contact 58
   N: Nod 59

CHAPTER 4: SMALL TALK AS A FIRE STARTER 61
CONVERSATION STARTERS 61
EFFECTIVE STRATEGIES TO START A CONVERSATION 62
   Release Shame with the Mask Technique 62
   Don't Forget the Goal 63
   Smile and the World Will Smile at You 64
   Prepare the Ground with a Simple Phrase 65
   Ask Something Related to the Situation or Place 66
   Show Curiosity About What They're Doing 67
   Give a Compliment and Continue with a Question 67
   Ask for a Recommendation, Advice, or Opinion 68
   Fill in Information Gaps 69
   Give a Way Out and Avoid Rejection 70
   Why It Can Fail 71
   Practice, Practice, and Practice 72
   Learn How to Start Deepening the Conversation 72

CHAPTER 5: ESTABLISHING A DEEP CONNECTION 75
PROPOSE A PERSONAL TOPIC 76
BREAKING THE ICE: AVOIDING EXCESSIVELY BANAL GREETINGS 76
RAISE QUESTIONS ABOUT YOUR LIFE AND EXPERIENCES 78
TRY TO ESTABLISH A TRUE RELATIONSHIP 78
DISCOVER YOUR GOALS AND DREAMS 79
TAKE AN INTEREST IN YOUR FAMILY 79
ASK QUESTIONS ABOUT YOUR PROFESSION INSTEAD OF YOUR JOB .. 80
REMEMBER YOUR PREVIOUS CONVERSATIONS 81
ASK OPEN-ENDED QUESTIONS 82
FOLLOW UP WITH DEEPER QUESTIONS 83
FIND COMMON INTERESTS AND EXPERIENCES 84
DISCOVER THE PREFERENCES OF OTHERS 85
STAY READY TO BE VULNERABLE 86
GIVE AND ASK FOR ADVICE 87
SHOW THAT YOU CARE ABOUT THE OTHER 88
CONSIDER HOW YOU CAN ADD VALUE TO THE CONVERSATION 88
DO WHAT CAN HELP YOU 89

- LISTEN INSTEAD OF PLANNING YOUR RESPONSE 90
- RECOGNIZE WHAT YOU JUST HEARD 91
- DISPLAYS OPEN BODY LANGUAGE 92
- ADDRESS THE CONVERSATION OPENLY 93
- IDENTIFY EACH PERSON AND INTEGRATE THEM INTO THE CONVERSATION 93
- COPY THE GOOD SPEAKERS 94
- SINCERITY 94
- ADMIT SOME OF YOUR PAST FAILURES 94
- DON'T MULTITASK WHILE TALKING TO SOMEONE 95
- DEVELOP THE CONVERSATION PATIENTLY 95
- SHOW GRATITUDE TO THE OTHER 96

CONCLUSION 97

Introduction

For years, I have dedicated myself to work on people's social skills. A decade guarantees my work. I have dedicated myself to communication and helping others communicate effectively.

Don't think this one you see here was always like this, I know first-hand what it's like to be introverted. For a long time, I had that fear, the trembling legs when trying to talk to another, the one who ran away from the party, the one who sat in a corner with a glass in his hand, wishing deep down that he was standing, with the other men, talking, seeing the women, listening, and being able to address issues naturally.

But, I felt like I was inside a steel box and couldn't get out of it, it's a challenge to be introverted in social situations. Now, I managed it and I want to help you.

My interest in communication started in my college days when I was also interested in human behavior.

Back then, I struggled to make friends and get the attention of girls, I had a weakness for popular girls. They seemed so relaxed in their manner all the time and I seemed stiff.

But one day, I stopped playing the victim and started to improve my social skills.

I studied psychology and communication and from then, until today, I have continued to study, practice and apply this knowledge.

That is why through my studies and personal experience, I have developed work for you to improve your introversion and social skills.

If you are one of those people who feel insecure about your value but you know deep down that you are worth a lot, but fear and many other thoughts make you remain hermetic and closed, you are not alone.

You don't have to condemn yourself to be this way if you have gone to classes, parties, or meetings and you are in the neutral zone. Where no one sees because you don't participate, and you have a hard time striking up a conversation with strangers.

Don't worry.

I'll help you get there. I will help you take action. Don't feel alone or helpless anymore, learn to overcome your fears of socializing with the steps you will learn in this book.

If you have the desire to make friends and be perceived as charming, empathetic, and open to deep conversations, you're in the right place.

No longer envy those who converse naturally, be one of them with the chapters where I've laid out the process for you to do so.

Become aware that you deserve a quality of life where you can express yourself and communicate like the best.

Become a brilliant and entertaining speaker.

In the following pages, you will learn how to be a good conversationalist in social contexts, overcoming that awkwardness and shyness that sometimes freezes you to engage in dialogue with others.

In addition, you will use conversation to establish solid and deep connections with new people, whether they are dates, friends, or business.

Few things scare an introvert more than being invited to a party. Things can get even worse if the party is likely to be full of strangers.

As a distinguished member of the introvert club, I have found myself in this situation on numerous occasions.

I admit that certain social events used to be a torment to me until I figured out why.

Introverts are not necessarily misanthropes. So, why would we rather go to the dentist than get an invitation to a party?

Well, because of the conversation. Most of our everyday conversations are superficial, barely above the level of "elevator conversation."

Questions like: "What do you do for a living?" "Where do you live?" or "Where do you plan to travel on your next vacation?" are usually general, but for that reason, they are just as repetitive and rambling.

They also do not serve to deepen our relationship and, on top of that, they end up being quite boring.

No one is completely introverted or extroverted and, in general, almost everyone falls somewhere between these two extremes, with one style or the other predominating.

One stance is neither better nor more appropriate than the other, and in many cases, it depends on the specific situation and context.

What matters is that each individual can adopt the attitude that best suits him or her about others and the world.

If we base ourselves on the biological part of these factors, contrary to what might be suspected beforehand, we find that introverts have a state of permanent excitement or alertness.

On the other hand, extroverts tend to have an activation of a more inhibited brain state.

But if the plan is to be able to take a trivial conversation, the one that is so hard to lengthen to make it deep and from there create connections, this is the right book.

I will explain specifically, well documented and with empirical experience, how to work on introversion, shyness, and what makes you not give way to good conversations.

I will help you understand that even if you think being introverted is bad, it turns out that it has more advantages than you imagine.

How to be a good observer, see more of what others don't realize when they talk, and be good leaders according to studies I'll show you ahead, at the end of the day, being introverted is not bad.

You just need that little tweak to make you take the step to speak up and here I will show you how.

Chapter 1: The Right Mindset, a New Framework for Thinking About Yourself

The first step to overcome shyness and regain your security is to become aware of what you think of yourself, what you say to yourself, and how you do it, and see yourself there, with that social phobia before others, preferring to flee than start a conversation from scratch. Therefore, let's talk about the phrases that limit you, how to empower yourself, and talk with total safety.

As You Feel Inside, You Project Outside

From the point of view of physics, everything in the universe is made of energy vibrating at a certain frequency. Of course, so do we. Mystics, on the other hand, claim that the more our consciousness grows, the higher the frequency of energy we vibrate as human beings, and viceversa. In fact, there is a very close correlation between our level of vital energy and our level of intelligence. I mean, if you create an energy of insecurity, everything around will look insecure, remember that moment when you felt safe, something happened to you that empowered you, you went out on the street and you felt that the whole world was this way with you, they saw you differently, but the next day, everything was as usual. It's because you projected that secure energy.

What happens when we're in a bad mood and stay up all night? What is our mood when we wake up in the morning? What thoughts go through our minds when we are stressed and tired? On the contrary, when we have slept a deep and restful sleep, what is our state of mind when we wake up? What is our habitual attitude toward life when we feel connected and energized? What thoughts visit us when we are calm and relaxed?

In other words, our mind is like a radio that can tune into different stations. When our energy levels are low, our minds tune in to "FM ignorance." On this dial, our thoughts vibrate at a lower frequency and are associated with fear, anger, sadness, and negativity. On the other hand, when our energy levels are high, our minds tune in to the "wisdom melody." On this dial, our mind has a high vibrational frequency and is associated with confidence, serenity, joy, and positivity.

Despite all this scientific and spiritual evidence, most of us don't consider this subtle but vibrant layer. Mainly because it is invisible to the naked eye. Therefore, we only see the physical and material part that covers it. Proof of this is our tendency to focus on physical symptoms rather than the mental causes that produce them. It is this frequency of internal energy that largely determines the reason for our external reality. This is something that has been expressed in different ways at different times in history, I do not want to go down that line, but maybe we will tear it a little so that you understand it.

As it is inside, it is outside. This statement comes from the Kybalion, a text dating from the nineteenth century that describes the principles and laws that govern the universe, whose metaphysics is related to the teachings of Hermes Trismegistus. Essentially, it means that our inner world generates our outer world. By what is happening to us externally (visible), we can recognize what is happening to us internally (invisible).

For example, think about why you are reading these reflections on how to reprogram your mind. Isn't it because you need a change in your heart? Do you have an open enough mind to go deeper into your being with this content? If this interests you and curiosity exists within you, your outer self at this time will have to be on more than just the journey of self-knowledge. In fact, if you go back a few years, you wouldn't even have imagined that one day you would consume this kind of information.

If You Believe It, You Believe It

What you believe is what you are. Our belief systems guide us to co-create our reality. If you think that you will go unnoticed, that no one will see you, so it will be, if you think you can be the center of attention and others will listen to you, so it will be. Of course, added body language and some ingredients that I will teach you later.

By believing that you have the power to change your life, you are creating this moment and you are absorbing the information on how to do it. If you didn't think about it, you wouldn't be able to be reading this book now. In addition, when you verify that this content is useful and true, you will begin to co-create another type of reality from the new information inserted into your belief system.

If you change, your life will change. No doubt this is one of the tritest mantras in the field, but not for nothing it has its truth. It says that when we question our beliefs, modify our thoughts, and reprogram our subconscious, we are slowly changing our attitude in life. As a direct consequence, the results we reap begin to change, both inside and outside of us.

Disempowering Phrases that Limit

If you are one of the people who say phrases that subtract power, such as "I am wrong every time I speak", "I freeze and do not know what else to say", or "I am afraid that they will listen to me" because, as I spoke in the previous subchapter, is what will happen to you, everyone will see you like that and ignore you. Disempowering phrases do their job well, they take away your power.

In the long run, this generates social phobia that affects emotions and is characterized by fear of relating to others. Taken to the extreme it is classified within anxiety disorders and medically is known as pathological social anxiety.

I'm not saying you have it, but among the many phobias, when that shyness gets out of control, you can end up like that.

People with this disorder have difficulties coping with gatherings or social gatherings because they fear ridicule or embarrassing experiences. First of all, you should know that fear is natural. We are all afraid of certain things: accidents, certain animals, infections, disasters, and situations.

Fear is a useful defense mechanism for survival because it involves prudent behavior so as not to experience something we don't want. Fear can help us a lot to stay safe in our daily lives and prevent situations that could be harmful to us. Fear is necessary for life as long as it does not limit us.

We face a phobia when fear becomes a problem, when it controls us. A phobia is an extreme fear of something that arises when the intensity of the fear we experience becomes extreme and leads us to make unnecessary preventive decisions.

The irrational fear of meeting other people is known as social phobia. When this fear of social contact is unreasonable because it precedes a stimulus, or is overwhelming for the scale of the experience, we must seek help. Healthy living and rewarding social sharing are possible, we just have to find a way to make it happen.

People with social phobia experience fear, insecurity, and a sense of danger; The same problems are present in any anxiety disorder, although in this case, they will become visible. As people with social phobia approach the time when they have to be in contact with a group of people (friends, co-workers, strangers, or even close people), they begin to experience a certain tension that, depending on the severity of the problem, if left unattended, can last a lifetime.

This discomfort can lead people to cancel commitments and adopt an attitude of isolation to avoid the situation. If you decide to face a horrific encounter, the experience will take an extremely high emotional toll.

Characteristics of Someone Afraid to Socialize

Social phobia starts early in life but is often detected early in adult life due to changes in personality development and often early erratic behavior. However, the root of the problem is usually identified in the early years and usually coincides with the start of school and the first social commitments outside the family environment.

Children who have experienced violence from their parents or elders may develop a great fear of interpersonal relationships. This is because, in the face of an abusive or overly stressful experience, their response is an act of withdrawal, which gradually convinces them that the best way to stay safe is to be alone, to be a shadow.

Detecting this type of behavior early on is critical to preventing the development of social phobia in the future.

Why Does It Appear?

While there is no specific answer to define why this phobia develops, since we are all different, some common experiences for people with this phobia is to have a very structured childhood in which they accepted to receive a rigorous education and were highly valued for the level of expectations placed on their shoulders.

The possibility of being seen as negative, incompetent, or unqualified by others stresses them out so much that it blocks them emotionally and makes it difficult for them to cope with social situations.

Is Shyness a Social Phobia?

I think it is important to say that when we talk about social phobia we do not mean shyness. The latter is related to a personality trait that sometimes hinders certain situations of social interaction, but in most cases is not considered pathological because it does not affect the quality of life of the individual. Or it affects it to a point that can be treated as we will in this book.

Social phobia, on the other hand, is an emerging disorder that, if left untreated, increases, hinders, and severely worsens the social relationships of a person with the disorder. Sometimes the symptoms of this irrational fear are interpreted as part of a shy or introverted personality, leading many people to justify their isolation and social restrictions without realizing that they have a social phobia problem. Therefore, it is necessary to know how to distinguish shyness from phobias.

When something happens to us that hinders and distorts some aspect of our life, we must pay attention to it because it means that things are not going well. In the case of social phobia, it is a disorder that hinders the healthy development of a person. It is also a problem that seriously interferes with the full enjoyment of their social life.

Therefore, if you fear or feel that you are suffering from it, you should seek professional help to see and treat yourself, addressing the problem promptly and being able to improve your quality of life.

Like most types of anxiety disorders, social phobia can seriously worsen our relationships because its characteristic irrational fears create in us the desire or need to isolate ourselves to avoid feeling bad or ashamed.

The insecurities are so strong that sometimes the only viable way out is to refuse exposure and opt for isolation. The decision to isolate ourselves reduces anxiety in the short term, but over time it can wreak havoc on our social relationships. Lockdown is seen as a desperate decision, but it can lead to distorted perceptions of reality and affect our intimate relationships.

That's because if some situation threatens us, tension will be reactivated, it will be difficult to keep all aspects of our lives organized, and our closest relationships will inevitably suffer.

You should know that sometimes social phobia can lead to other problems, such as alcoholism. Many people, fearing exposure, decide to drink alcohol to release their inhibitions and be able to face social situations. This could be a temporary solution, but it can cause serious problems for the victim in the long run. The social need to drink is a double problem that is difficult to solve. Social phobia combined with alcoholism complicates intimate relationships and makes it an adventure to find a partner and new friends, among other consequences.

Reframing Insecure Thoughts

Our insecurities bring out the best in us, but other times they hinder our growth. We have doubts about how we look, how we speak, what we can do, our talents, or our actions, in short, any issue that accuses us because it is the product of lost trust.

Self-esteem is affected. Stopping our insecurities is not easy because we are born with the fear of being judged or rejected, but it is not impossible. I want to leave you some tips that can help you restore your integrity and your desire to relate without being afraid to do so. Here it is about insecurity, and how to overcome it.

Introspect at the Origin of Insecurities

We may have personal insecurities from childhood or adolescence, although many of us manage to overcome them in adulthood and as we reach our life goals, not always it's like that. Insecurity often has a severe impact on self-confidence and self-esteem, as well as relationships with others.

To end once and for all the ghosts that limit our success and happiness, we must first recognize what their causes are and why they still exist within us. Some of the most common reasons why a person cannot overcome fear are:

Relationship with Parents

Everyone's attachment relationship with their parents greatly affects their sense of security and begins in childhood, when people develop attachment styles. Trauma from neglect, rejection, or abuse is a common cause, depending on the meaning of insecurity. If there was not a good socialization relationship with the parents, if they despised them or made them feel insecure, that may be where the shyness to speak arises.

Social Anxiety

It can arise in childhood for many reasons, including peer rejection, parental pressure, bullying, discrimination, or other traumatic events. Anxiety can distort someone's perception of themselves and fear being constantly evaluated.

Recent Failures

We are all prone to failure, but these situations usually trigger those of us who grew up with certain insecurities. People who lack self-confidence tend to be more sensitive to setbacks and failures. This is the case of the loss of a loved one, divorce, dismissal, etc.

Perfectionism

Some people carry the need to get things done and succeed to such an extent that they are picky about details and when they fail, their frustration levels can skyrocket, leading to depression and insecurity. We can pour all our effort and energy into every purpose and still not be infallible.

Challenge Negative Thoughts

You won't overcome your insecurities if you keep belittling yourself and repeating your failures. Self-criticism is often our worst enemy, as it traps our mind in states of pessimism and guilt that are often insurmountable. If you want to overcome your fear, it's time to rethink your way of thinking, the way you communicate with yourself will contribute to your success or failure, simple as that. To start reversing the thought patterns that overwhelm you, we recommend taking the following steps to eliminate insecurities:

Record Bad Thoughts

This will allow you to know how many times a day and why your mind turns to negative thoughts so that you can control and avoid them, replacing them with images that fill you with confidence and mental balance. The first step to eliminating insecurities.

Ask Yourself Questions

When a bad or pessimistic thought arises, ask yourself a series of questions like if you were a reporter, including what caused a bad thought, when it came up, if it was helpful, and if it happened to someone else what advice would you give to them? Think of another insecure person, who you see wanting to talk, or when they do it is not the best and you can tell that they are nervous, what would you say to that person, then you say the same thing to you?

Be Realistic

Most perceptions of reality are distorted by frightening thoughts. Emotions or feelings often prevent people from evaluating facts truly and fairly. You must consider how much reality or fantasy your insecurities or doubts accumulate.

Look for Different Perspectives

Finding out which recurring negative thoughts visit you give you a huge advantage. You can decide to avoid them, but you can also transform them into useful, successful, and joyful thoughts and ideas. Seeing it as a challenge to face that fear of talking to others. Shift your approach from things that can go wrong to scenarios with an optimistic narrative.

Embrace the Uncomfortable

Successful people know how to laugh at themselves, they see failure as a challenge and an opportunity to continue learning that the world does not end there. The next time you're stuck and feel like a failure or self-conscious, instead of thinking about yourself, see some of the achievements and mistakes you'll have to overcome to get it right next time. At the same time, you accept other people's opinions in a constructive way, rather than taking them as personal attacks, because even then, you can only filter out what other people's reviews can do better for you and discard those that aren't good. When you think about running away from a conversation, stop, face fear, and take the step, even if it does not go well, practice until you get it. Fight with the thoughts that disempower and change them with "yes, I can, I am the best speaker, and I have a lot to tell."

Accept Errors

We are all prone to failure and misbehaving. No one is infallible or perfect. Making mistakes is part of every learning process, and you should enjoy it as much as possible.

Don't Push Yourself So Hard

As the saying goes, we can all do everything, but not everything at the same time. Go one step at a time and don't get overwhelmed by meeting unrealistic standards, whether yours or someone else's. Sometimes the first attempt does not go well and we have to learn to accept and work with our limitations. Have compassion for yourself. Do not give up, but do not pressure yourself if you do not do well in the first ones.

Broaden the Picture

This is where that need to be perfect comes into play, and if you care a lot about details and doubts, you will end up distracted from your important goals. Remember that mistakes can be overcome, and the important thing is that you stop punishing yourself and move forward thinking about your future.

Don't Compare Yourself

This is one of the worst mistakes everyone makes insecurely. Social comparison trends that spread easily from social media tend to leave us dissatisfied and disappointed with ourselves. Remember, not all that shines are gold, and we, as spectators, only glimpse the spectacle of other people's lives. Many times, those who are cheerful and noisy in an environment, hide depression, and monsters that stalk them, do not envy them, work to develop, and know how to socialize, from the inside out.

Try

Failure is possible, but only if we give ourselves to success, and as long as we have the will, we can grow, even beyond our fears, uncertainties, and insecurities. Instead of getting bored with counterproductive thoughts, like why I'm so unsure about my partner, visualize yourself getting closer to your goals and improving your relationship.

List Your Strengths and Qualities

We insist that you must have compassion for yourself and be your best friend, a friend who understands you, forgives you, praises you, and affirms your value. It is a remarkable exercise to overcome our anxieties and insecurities and take stock of everything we do well and the small decisions we make every day that give us fulfillment and satisfaction. We all have things to be proud of.

Think about those qualities or traits that make you brag, it doesn't have to be a physical attribute, it can be your gifts or character traits. Make a list of these good things, preferably in writing, and don't forget at least five of them, it will help you get rid of your insecurities.

If you don't know what to do, lean on your friends and family and ask them what virtues they see in you. You may be pleasantly surprised, nothing like being surrounded by people who love and understand you, increase your confidence, and make you feel accepted for who you are.

ite of negativity and confusion for long periods found effect on our lives. At first, it is inevitable immediate damage to our physical and mental f-esteem is easy to manifest, and it also makes us give up our dreams, succumb to our comfort zone and stagnate. Insecurity can also affect our relationships, in which we trust our frustration, anger, and distrust toward friends, partners, or family. All that said, stopping your insecurities is something you need to seriously address first, to save once and for all the opportunities for advancement and fulfillment that life offers you.

Techniques for Approaching Conversations If You're Shy

With this in mind, I want to propose a few ideas that can help you break the ice and start conversations with new people without being so afraid.

Acknowledge Your Shyness

If it is our shyness that worries us, it is best to admit it. There are more shy people than you think, and affirming this can allow you to bond with yourself, empathize with shy people and make your evenings more enjoyable with more extroverted people. Accept it with humor, laughing, and saying that so that you don't get alienated, but see yourself as a genuine person and therefore funny.

Make a Compliment

A good way to break the ice is to bet on starting a conversation with a compliment, as long as it is believable. So, if we have just met that person, it is better to only comment on their physical appearance, say that we like their watch or any other accessory, or agree and be interested when that person thinks or tells us an "anecdote" story.

Appeal to the Classic

There are immortal classics, I don't know what to say, as long as we don't start talking about time, we can pull them off. The proposals are simple, such as "Where are you from?", which allows people to tell something about themselves, and "What do you do?" Also, the most emotional topics are usually easy to deal with, such as talking about a trip that we love. Another idea is to remember the news, for example, talk about the latest premiere on a billboard or a famous television program.

Smile and Make Eye Contact

It's not just what we say, but how we say it. Luisa Pilar Modroño has not forgotten the importance of "smiling and looking into the eyes to give a sense of openness." In addition, another important point is to practice what is called "active listening," which consists of "maintaining eye contact intermittently, nodding, agreeing (if any) with what you are telling us, or summarizing in a sentence what you are seeing." Such as: So, you like to spend summers on the beach?

Answer with Questions

If once a topic arises, we want to continue the conversation instead of falling back into an awkward silence, another approach is to respond with questions rather than cutting sentences that can end the conversation. Having open-ended questions also allows the other person to give a broader answer than yes or no, so we provide opportunities to deepen or open new topics.

Respect Each Other's Space

The tension in this situation often causes us to make mistakes, such as speaking too loud or fast, gesticulating too much or even violating the other person's space, so we give the wrong feeling. In this regard, I recommend you be very respectful of the space of the person we are talking to and be careful not to push too hard.

Dose Personal Information

When we don't know someone and want to strike up a conversation, of course, we also provide information about ourselves, but we have to learn to control it a little. Asking for and providing personal information is a great resource, but we should never overdo it with very intimate details that may make the other person feel uncomfortable or questionable. We can always change it by directing the conversation to other more objective or light topics.

Listen Before You Speak

The good thing about being shy is that being quiet allows you to observe a lot, which can be an advantage when socializing with new people. Therefore, it is important to pay attention to the content of the group discussion, such as the taste for music or cinema. In this way, we can find common ground and weave the conversation around it, always asking positive questions about tastes and interests. It is not only listening but also observing. Although appearances sometimes deceive, carrying a Batman phone case can tell us something about each other, and can also become a haven for topical conversations.

Avoid Controversial Topics

When we don't know the people, we interact with, it's good to consider what topics should and shouldn't be mentioned because it's best to avoid controversial topics, such as politics or religion. We don't know the tendencies of the people present... Unless we are sure that they will not cause us any conflict, it is best to avoid them.

Don't Lie

It may seem like a cliché, but the phrase "be yourself" is still good advice in these situations, what is never recommended is to lie and pretend that we are not who we are. It will only make things worse for you and those around you.

Learn How to Overcome Shyness with These Steps

We all have insecurities to one degree or another because life teaches us that not all experiences are pleasant and that many situations are beyond our control. Here I leave you exercises that you can use in facing that shyness.

Speak Without Fear of Insecurity, Do Not Put Masks or Hide It

When it comes to managing our insecurities, we can do it positively (I accept my weaknesses, I can talk about them, I work to change them, so I mature) or in a negative way (disguising them through jealousy, blackmail, harassment, abuse, etc.). It is appropriate to state out loud our insecurities as we work to change what is hurting us, for example: "I am insecure because I do not know how to speak fluently, but little by little I am becoming more confident and I am liking myself more and more and so I talk to others", "I get very nervous when I speak in a meeting, so I have to work hard and not feel inferior to others", "I'm afraid to talk to that person, but I spend half an hour practicing every day in front of the mirror," etc.

Go Back to Thoughts That Cause You Insecurity

There are countless erroneous thoughts, what we call distorted thoughts, which are characterized by being involuntary, and automatic, that arise from time to time, in the moments when we are depressed. First of all, recognize them, realize their irrationality, and then begin to debate them and change them for another philosophy of life. Some of these thoughts can be:

"No one loves me," "No one finds me interesting," "Everyone speaks badly of me," "I can't achieve anything in my life," or "It's not worth being a human being."

Work Healthy Selfishness

Although in society we are taught that the word egoistic is associated with negative things, being selfish in a healthy way is necessary to value yourself. We have to pay attention to how we feel, what we want, and what we need and then, if we want, also meet the needs of others. Let's go first, then the others.

Express Your Thoughts and Feelings

Say what you think and feel in the first person. Don't be afraid to have conflicts or bad opinions. Pay attention to your feelings and the fear will disappear. We can confidently say anything we want without disrespecting the other person. This will allow us to identify with the personality we are developing and increase our self-confidence.

Value Yourself, Love Yourself, Take Care of Yourself

Start by valuing everything about yourself. Write down who you are, your weaknesses, and your strengths on a piece of paper, and take some time to think only about your strengths. Other exercises can be the following: allow yourself to walk into a restaurant and order a dish that you like, no matter how much it costs, or how fattening it is... Reward yourself just because you like it. Try to find evidence against those very negative thoughts you have about yourself, for example, if you think you are a bad parent, stop and think about all those situations in which you acted like a good parent and write them down on a piece of paper. Take a bath with aromatic salts after a stressful day at work. Do not punish yourself, allow yourself to enjoy and take care of yourself.

Learn to Say No and Make Decisions Based on It

Dare to reject other people's suggestions or ideas, but don't defend yourself too much. This way, others will know that you have limits and will not blackmail or manipulate you. Make decisions based on what you want, and how you feel and live with its consequences. Although it seems strange at first, it is normal. Live with it and you will discover how little by little you will feel freer and safer.

Don't Compare Yourself to Others

The goal is to increase self-confidence, to be who you are, not who you are with other people. Don't compare yourself to those you think are better than you because while that's not a bad thing in itself, it can make you feel inferior at the moment. For example, "If you got a 7 on an exam, you would be sad to know that many of your classmates got 8, 9, or 10. The ones who got 6 and 5, would you consider them? Does it count?" Another example is, "I look fat, and I feel bad because I see other muscular people on the street. So, people who weigh more than you or are even obese, pass your evaluation?"

Act As If

In theater, it's a great tool for playing different roles. Create a character that is safe and how you want it and give it life in your day to day. Acting "as if" will make change come faster. This may seem silly, but it is a very effective and reliable technique. Act like you're a confident person, as you like yourself, like you love your physique, like you look good. Act like you like to drive, like you're happy to see your boss, like you're talking to others with that confidence. A false version of yourself, but verbalizing changes in how you look (or want to look) so that, little by little, your way of thinking changes. First, we act "as if" we are safe beings, and then we verbalize it so that, subsequently, our thoughts align with our new vision of ourselves.

Dare for New Things

Do things that are challenging for you that involve stepping out of your familiar bubble (comfort zone) where you control everything. New things, things that scare you, things that mean change. Cut your hair, go floating, put on flashy clothes, paint your lips red, meet that person who you are embarrassed to meet, taste Indian food, whatever it is, dare! Only then, you will understand that you are more capable than you imagine of doing beautiful things that bring you joy and confidence.

The plan is that you work to achieve a safe mentality, that if you see phrases that take away your power, change them to powerful and repeat them many times so at the beginning do not believe them. Reframe those insecure thoughts and make affirmations of moderation, repetition, and practice that will cause you to inoculate them in you.

In the next chapter, I will talk about how introversion can be a weapon for you, learning to be a great observer, and taking data to be able to converse with others from your position.

Chapter 2: Introversion as the Strongest Conversational Weapon

We saw in the previous chapter how to not be insecure and how those phrases that steal your power limit you, now, I want to work on accepting what you are but using it to your advantage.

Extroverts Have a Reputation for Being Good Leaders

Shy, quiet, asocial, and even fearful (to say the least) are some (fake) labels that millions of introverts in today's world still accept.

In a culture where team meetings or job interviews are more like a competition for the more talkative and charisma is the golden rule, it seems wrong to be less open to socializing.

If you are an introvert, you are sure to know how complex it is to deal with a world (from your childhood experiences) where everything seems to be designed for people with more interpersonal and communication skills. It's something that seems to be getting stronger.

Extroverts are often given more weight during the group selection process or even in jobs, especially during interviews. And an introverted candidate is often classified as a poor choice because of their limited public interaction skills.

Although in recent years employers have realized the importance of diversity and are gradually incorporating it into their selection process, there is still a long way to go!

The strength of introverts is overshadowed by stereotypes or misconceptions, which hinder their development and career advancement.

Does Introversion Equal Shyness?

No, being introverted is not the same as being shy. Shyness is the fear of social judgment. But what is an introvert? According to the RAE, someone is said to be an introvert if they have "difficulty in social relationships" and are "introverted."

However, I must specify something in this definition: the difficulty to relate at the social level occurs in large groups of people.

Introverts also focus their interest on their "inner world" formed by their feelings, reflections, and thoughts, which, according to experts, "makes them more empathetic." But there is much more!

Characteristics of Introverts

So, if introverts aren't shy or asocial, what are their characteristics? "They are people who love to listen, people who like to innovate and create, but they don't promote themselves; People who like to work alone and don't like to work in a team."

When they are in quieter and less stimulating environments, they feel more alive, energetic, and empowered. Unlike extroverts who work best in shared spaces where collaborative workflows, introverts need places without much noise and distractions to focus and spark their creativity.

According to Harvard Business Review, introverts have more energy when they are alone.

Introverted people also tend to have an active imagination and a busy mind. Studies mention a correlation between creativity and introversion, the truth is that not all creative people are introverts, and not all introverts are creative. Still, facts tend to tip the scales toward the correlation between innovative thinking and introverted thinking.

Some famous introverts of our time are:

- Albert Einstein, the most important physicist of the twentieth century.

- Amancio Ortega, the owner of Inditex (Zara).

- Bill Gates, the founder of Microsoft.

- Jeff Bezos, the creator of Amazon.

- Mark Zuckerberg, the creator of Facebook.

As an Introvert, There Is a Lot You Can Give

We tend to assume being in other spaces we must project an image of being enthusiastic, extroverted, confident, and clearly oriented.

But in reality, what may require a particular position are the traits and skills of a talented introvert.

You Can Be a Great Leader

Extroverts excel in any standard professional situation because they are more likely to connect with people. After all, soft skills are highly valued, and because we believe they find it easier to lead or sell. However, this social convention that leaders should be more dominant, and outgoing is not as poetic as it is painted.

In some situations, introverted leaders may be more effective than extroverted leaders. The key is who those leaders lead.

Grant and Harvard Business School researchers Francesca Gino and David Hofmann of the University of North Carolina's Kenan-Flagler School of Business studied a company with 130 stores, 57 store managers, and 374 employees.

Here's what the research turned up:

- When employees are proactive, introverted managers drive them to higher profits.

- When employees are not proactive, extroverted managers lead to higher profits.

Why Is This Happening?

Interestingly, neither introverted nor extroverted leaders proved to be more productive or profitable than the other group. The only difference lies in the combination between leader and collaborator.

Ultimately, introverted and extroverted leadership styles are highly effective, and the determining factor is the combination of the above. This means that companies need to balance their teams by hiring introverts and extroverts and bringing them together in ways that they can understand and integrate.

As an Introvert, You Can Practice Active Listening and Mindful Observation

Listening is an essential part when communicating. Listening means paying the necessary attention to understand the message being sent. The goal of active listening is to get as much information as possible to understand people before you start responding.

Listening is an active process that requires conscious effort, concentration, and interest and involves both physical and mental effort. For this reason, not everyone is equipped to provide active listening, as it requires work and sometimes training.

Active listening is difficult to achieve because it requires a certain level of attention and means actively absorbing the information received, which often does not happen naturally. Active listening does not exist in isolation, it must be complemented with a set of soft skills such as emotional intelligence or empathy that will make active listening more effective and authentic.

Among the cognitive characteristics of active listening, is paraphrasing and summarizing what is heard. Ask questions to gain a deeper understanding of a situation and gain a clearer understanding of the topic being discussed.

Knowing how to communicate is not only talking, listening is crucial both inside and outside the workplace, and active listening is the most important form of communication.

The process involves seeing a message, understanding the meaning hidden in it, and then crafting a response by showing that you are engaged and retained the message.

Active listening in different environments means paying attention and being in tune with what's going on around you. It helps you accumulate more information and understand it better, allowing you to make better decisions and respond more appropriately to situations.

Active Listening Techniques

- Maintain eye contact with the other person.

- Pay full attention to the person issuing the message.

- Correct posture and body movements based on focus and attention to the sender.

- Positive verbal reinforcement to the other party.

Active Listening Dynamics

Choosing different team dynamics in companies to improve certain skills or simply to help employees get to know each other and interact with each other is nothing new. In this case, the dynamics of active listening aim to improve this quality in employees.

So we can point out several dynamics designed for this purpose:

- Dynamics of taking turns talking. It helps to get people's opinions on a particular topic.

- The dynamic contradiction of thought. Starting with a topic, participants develop critical thinking and contractions about it.

- Dynamic human bridge. Practice understanding how information is distorted from person to person.

Active listening is an essential skill for today's leaders. Knowing what it means and how to incorporate it into our character is a key value to being a better leader every day and facing the challenges foreseen both in the workplace and personally.

The Active Listening Study Technique is a very useful and effective resource to understand how to act and work on a day-to-day basis with active listening in our environment.

Do you think you know how to listen? Let's take a look. Here are some questions, please answer as honestly as possible. Think that when you have a conversation with a friend or family member, you have to listen to the other person:

- Do you think about your answer while the other is talking?

- Do you guess what he's going to say before he speaks or finishes?

- Do you cut him to express your opinion or to finish his sentences? (given your case it should be less likely)

- Do you disconnect or get distracted by thinking about other topics?

- Do you react impulsively to certain words?

If you answered yes to the three questions above, I strongly advise you to be vigilant with this part of the book.

We define active listening as the ability to listen to the message sent to us by the sender, making a conscious and voluntary effort to pay attention, follow the thread of the conversation, and understand in depth what he is telling us. It's not just about listening to what he told us, keeping them in working memory, but about understanding the full message.

To put this skill into practice it is necessary to focus on the person with whom we are talking, avoiding distractions and trying to offer counterarguments while the other person continues to talk. If we are distracted thinking about how to reproduce it, it is impossible to understand everything they are telling us, because in doing so we begin to ignore parts of the message they are trying to share.

It takes a lot of focus and determination to be able to play the role of an active listener. It's complicated, but not impossible, because while breaking old habits is hard and consciously avoiding distractions is a real challenge, it's perfectly feasible to maximize your attention on those who share your thoughts, emotions, and perspectives. As long as we actively participate in the practice of listening.

In general, we can say that the practice of active listening focuses on five areas to consider:

- Pay real attention
- Show that you listen
- Provide feedback
- Don't make value judgments while listening.
- Respond appropriately.

Active listening helps us to be better communicators. In addition, by listening better to what others tell us, we can create a more positive environment, avoid misunderstandings and reduce the likelihood of uncomfortable situations, such as having to repeat over and over again what we have already been told.

No one likes it when, after giving a speech, the people who are supposed to listen to them can't understand anything they say. Active listening is a sign of respect and appreciation. In your case of an introvert, silent, even seeming that you are not there, you listen and see others, you take data, know and know more than the one who invests a lot of time talking and talking.

Active Listening Exercises

Next, I leave you some active listening exercises that are excellent to improve this skill, it will be easy because by default you already have that:

View a Conversation

The first one I show you is the solo one. It may seem strange that active listening practice can be done without anyone, but the truth is that it is the best way to practice before encountering real human relationships where you need to demonstrate good listening skills. This exercise is ideal for practicing active listening.

Imagine you want to tell someone else how you spent your day yesterday (think about what you did; think about who you want to tell). Once you've decided on the theme and characters, move on. Now imagine how you tell it, what details you pay more attention to because you want to influence it, and what aspects you want to tell in depth.

Let's say they have been paying attention to what you've said, looking at you, smiling at you, making gestures based on the information you've said, expressing surprise at unexpected details, or sadness at unfortunate statistics. They have kept you in this world so that you can use your hair and gestures to explain what you want to convey to him.

Now imagine the opposite situation. This person gives a very different impression, interrupting you every time you say three words, constantly interrupting you. He gives you advice without you asking, even changes the subject, and gives you, his opinion.

How are you feeling? What kind of behavior do you prefer?

This is an exercise, although solitary and mental, of great help to put empathy into practice, how other people would feel if we did the same in a second situation.

The Bus

The bus game is a classic icebreaker activity in some places where it has not yet been done. The plan is simple, ask attendees to listen carefully to the story you are about to tell and, in the end, ask them a question:

Imagine you're driving a bus. At first, the bus is empty. At the first stop, five people go up. At the next stop, three people get off and two people go up. At this point, start telling how many passengers are in the car. Then, ten people went up and four went down. Finally, at the end of the line, five more passengers got off.

The question is: what foot size do bus users use?

When asking this question, it is not uncommon for the audience to be stereotyped, saying that it is impossible to know the answer. If this is the case, the statement should be repeated as much as necessary, until the participant arrives at an answer that can only be obtained by listening carefully to the exercise.

The answer is pretty simple (and fun): You're the bus driver, so you know what your shoe size is.

The Blind Man

Another group activity that we can put into practice is games for the blind. In this exercise, you can ask someone you trust to help you and you should act as "blind."

The activity consists of a blind person blindfolded leaving the room or field where the practice is going to be carried out, trying to avoid a series of obstacles such as tables, chairs, and cushions... to avoid injury or crashes. You must understand the instructions they give you.

The plan is to see the best time you throw yourself to overcome those obstacles, although that's not the main goal of the event. The main objective is that the person who plays the blind person follows active listening, paying close attention to what his peers say without distractions.

Selective Listening

Another valuable exercise is selective listening. For this activity ask several members of your family to help you and divide, one group A and another group B. Group A will be subdivided into A1 and A2 and a small story will be told that you have to pay close attention to as they will receive questions.

History can be anything, and also a slogan or slogan they say, as long as they are different. For example, you can ask group A1 to count the number of times the word "the" is said, while group A2 may be asked to count the number of times we say "one." An example story is the following, you will be a participant as a listener, which is what interests us about this, it is something that can also be applied individually to you.

A long time ago, in a village, there was a girl with brown hair and a red turban. Her mother asked her to bring a basket of food. The girl carried the basket happily through the woods, along the road that led to her grandmother's house. On the way she met a wolf who wanted to eat her, but the girl ran away because she was very hungry, so she ran to her grandmother's house and gave her the basket.

While groups A1 and A2 wait to see how many "the" and "one" occur in history, there is another group, group B. This group is only asked of one thing: they listened carefully to the story, that's all. We don't ask you to focus on anything in particular, so stay tuned while the story is told.

After telling the story, questions are asked related to what has just been told. Among these questions, we can say "What color is the girl's hair?" or "What's in the basket?" Here you see the difference between Group A and Group B.

Those in A, who have been waiting to keep track of words, will say they probably didn't realize what the story was about, while those in B, who were asked to listen, will find it easier to answer these questions.

Here we see the difference between selective listening (corresponding to what group A does) and applied active listening (in the case of group B).

Tell Me Your Story

This activity is done with three people. Each member will tell a story to the other in general terms, emphasizing details and events that are meaningful and important to the person telling them. Subsequently, each introduces another and tries to tell the same story he told them, trying to remember details and highlights.

Once the first step is done and all your stories told, there will be a debate, there will be a round of questions:

- Did you feel that the person has heard and understood you?

- How did you feel when you told your story and feelings?

- How did you feel when you had to tell your partner's story and reflect on what they felt?

- What was more complex: repeating or reflecting? Why?

- What do you take most important from the message?

- What do you learn from this experience?

This activity is designed to train attention, focusing on what is being said and the emotions that accompany telling another person's story. It also allows us to develop our empathy by trying to interpret with respect what other people have confessed to us.

Observe the Other Person's Appearance

In addition to practicing active listening, it is good that you work on your body language, which is something that we will see in the next chapter, but especially read that of others, their appearance, hobbies, and details they have, that will tell you a lot, because non-verbal communication talks more than what the words say and from your introversion, you can follow it. When you actively listen, also observe in detail.

Chapter 3: Body Language as Your Business Card

In the previous chapter, I talked about introverts and how you can take advantage of it by listening and observing actively, now, I want to talk about body language that you can use as a presentation, what the first impression is, and also, applying it with the S.O.F.T.E.N. technique that I explain in this chapter.

Nonverbal communication includes signs, gestures, and eye contact. Words do not necessarily have a place here, but they convey meaning. They can also be used to express enthusiasm for a particular topic. That's why body language is very important when you relate. Keep in mind, however, that nonverbal communication isn't limited to what you do in signs. Cultural differences can also cause communication problems. But I want us to focus on what you're going to observe and transmit.

When "communicate" is spoken, it usually refers to "what we say" or the words we use. Human communication, on the other hand, is much more than the literal meaning of words and the message or information they convey. It also includes behaviors that convey implicit messages, whether intentional or not, facial expressions, tone, intonation, and language gestures

Both the body (kinesiology) and the physical space between communicators are examples of nonverbal communication (relationship).

The technique of transmitting and receiving messages without using spoken or written language is known as nonverbal communication. Nonverbal behaviors can emphasize parts of verbal communication, just as italics emphasize written material.

Nonverbal information has been recognized as an important element of communication for decades. Francis Bacon said: "The five senses of the body generally reveal the disposition and tendency of the mind, but the movements of the face and parts reveal not only this but also the emotions and the present state... and the will of the mind.

Nonverbal communication is important in our lives because it enhances a person's ability to connect, engage, and form meaningful interactions in everyday life. If people have a better understanding of this style of communication, they can form deeper relationships with others.

The Impact of Nonverbal Language on Verbal Language

When looking at the relationship between verbal and nonverbal language, six ways in which nonverbal communication directly affects our spoken language have been identified.

To begin, we can use nonverbal signs to emphasize our comments. Someone who knows how to express himself and knows what to say, through forceful gestures, volume or speed adjustments, conscious pauses, etc. They can give messages that are not forgotten, for example, Obama made short silences when giving speeches, so that he could emphasize his messages.

The other point, what we say can be repeated through our nonverbal behavior. We can nod according to someone... For example, showing emotion in language along with the word.

Third, nonverbal cues can be used instead of words. Verbal expressions are not always necessary. A simple gesture (e.g., shaking your head to say no, thumbs up to say 'good job', etc.) Enough.

Types of Nonverbal Communication

Expressions on the Face

Much of the nonverbal communication is transmitted through the expressions of the face. Just think about how much information you can convey with a smile or a frown. Even before any word is released, surely you remember someone who came angry and you deduced it just by seeing it, we are usually the first to notice the look on a person's face.

Although communication and nonverbal language can vary widely between cultures, facial emotions such as happiness, sadness, anger, and fear are universal.

Gestures

Deliberate movement and signaling are important ways to convey meaning without the use of words. Greeting, pointing, and using your fingers to indicate values are common gestures. Other gestures are arbitrary and have a cultural basis.

In a court setting, lawyers have been known to use many nonverbal cues in an attempt to influence a jury's opinion. An attorney might look at your watch to imply that the opposing attorney's case is boring, or you might even roll your eyes in an attempt to discredit your witness statement.

Because nonverbal cues are considered so powerful and influential, some judges impose limits on the types of nonverbal behavior that can be used in court.

Paralinguistics

Speech communication that differs from actual language is known as paralinguistics. This includes things like pitch, volume, intonation, and tone of voice. Consider the importance of intonation in determining the meaning of a sentence.

When spoken in a strong tone, the audience can understand the praise and enthusiasm. Words spoken in a cautious tone can be interpreted as disdain and lack of interest.

Consider how changing intonation can change the meaning of a sentence in several ways. When a friend asks you how you're doing, you can respond with the traditional "I'm fine," but the way you say these words can reveal a lot about how you feel. If you say "I'm fine" with a sad face and a soft, muffled voice, it shows that you are not fine.

An indifferent tone could mean that you don't feel well, but don't want to talk about it. A cheerful and optimistic tone shows that you are doing fine.

Posture and Body Language

The way you stand and move can also say a lot. Body language research has come a long way since the 1970s, but the popular press has focused on excessive interpretations of defensive postures, crossed arms, and legs.

While nonverbal gestures like these can reveal feelings and attitudes, research shows that body language is much more subtle and less assertive than previously thought.

Proxemics

People often express their desire for "personal space," which is a form of nonverbal communication. Social conventions, cultural expectations, situational considerations, personality traits, and familiarity determine how far apart we should be and how much space we feel we have.

The amount of personal space needed for casual conversation with other people typically ranges from 18 inches to 4 feet. However, when talking to others, a personal distance of one meter is required.

Look with Your Eyes

Nonverbal communication has a lot to do with gaze, and nonverbal activities such as staring, staring, and blinking are common. When a person meets another or something they like, the blinking speed increases, and their pupils dilate. Seeing another can convey a variety of feelings, including hostility, intrigue, and attraction.

People also use their eyes to judge whether the other is telling the truth. Constant, normal eye contact is often interpreted as a sign that someone is telling the truth and can be trusted. On the other hand, cunning eyes and an inability to maintain eye contact are often interpreted as signs of deception or lying.

Appearance

Nonverbal communication is also influenced by our choices of colors, clothing, hairstyles, and other variables that affect appearance. Consider how many times you've made quick judgments about someone based on their appearance. First impressions are important, so according to experts, job candidates should dress appropriately when interviewing potential employers.

Research has found that how people look, as well as how much they earn, is affected by appearance. According to a 1996 survey, lawyers who considered themselves more handsome than their peers paid 15 percent more than others.

Culture has a huge impact on how people perceive the attractiveness of others. While thinness is valued in Western countries, in some African communities a plumper figure is associated with better health, wealth, and social status.

SOFTEN Technique and Non-Verbal Communication

Credibility is related to several different non-linguistic characteristics. Active violations of expectations are more likely to build trust than negative ones. These can be verbal and non-verbal. Based on previous research, the model can predict how people feel about other people. But its limitations include a lack of reliability. The study did not consider the effect of a person's emotions on trustworthiness.

Higher F1 scores corresponded to higher reliability, while lower F2 scores indicated greater tension and dominance. Conversely, lower F2 scores indicate greater ambivalence. The study also noted that looking up and leaning forward were positive indicators of reliability, but negative coefficients indicated low levels of these traits. This means that the level of trust in a relationship is less susceptible to nonverbal cues.

Nonverbal behaviors that positively correlated with trustworthiness were dominance, tension, and upright posture. In contrast, low F1 scores and high F2 scores were associated with lower levels of reliability. F1 scores correlated with higher research scores, but with lower overall accuracy. In addition, the relationship between these two characteristics and reliability was not as high as that of other characteristics.

What Does the SOFTEN Technique of Nonverbal Communication Mean?

In general, both men and women exhibit strong gender-related behaviors. Women are more likely than men to use nonverbal cues and have different levels of confidence. In other words, if they are authoritarian and neurotic, they are more likely to distrust them. Conversely, if they are more vulnerable, they are less likely to show their emotions.

F1 scores are associated with the highest level of reliability, while F2 scores are associated with the lowest. This difference suggests that these non-linguistic characteristics are not intrinsic components of the confidence rating. They may be the least important. But these traits are associated with perceived dominance and trustworthiness. Therefore, both men and women tend to use them. Most respondents believed that these nonverbal signals were sent unconsciously by their partners.

The results of this study demonstrate that the number of nonverbal characteristics related to trust has a positive relationship with positive F1. On the other hand, negative coefficients are related to low confidence. The same study found that the number of gazes, body inclination, and speed of speech were positive indicators of reliability. In other words, these signals can be used to assess the reliability of relationships.

What Is the F1 Score in the SOFTEN Technique?

The F1 score is the highest at 59%, but overall, this result is not significant. While the F1 score is the most accurate, averaging scores results in lower accuracy. It's also important to note that other nonverbal traits of confidence aren't directly related to mastery or poise. The average of the results shows that dominance and reliability are not easily predictable.

The F1 score has the highest correlation with confidence. The lowest correlations are nerve and dominance. F1 scored highest with a ratio of 0.7 to 0.9. F2 scored 59%, while F3 scored the lowest with a ratio of 0.8-0.9. In addition, sensitivity to the F1 score is lower and overall accuracy is lower.

Nonverbal communication can be both intentional and unintentional. Facial expressions are especially difficult to regulate because we can't see ourselves knowing what we're doing. As a result, we can confuse communication by consciously trying to convey one message and, without realizing it, conveying another.

Human communication is made more difficult by the fact that it is almost impossible to accurately analyze only gestures or expressions. Nonverbal communication consists of various expressions, hand and eye movements, postures, and gestures that must be interpreted along with language.

What Is the SOFTEN Technique?

The SOFTEN method involves nonverbal behavior to reduce any apprehension that interactors may have when initiating a new connection.

S: Smile

A smile is a sign of welcome. It transmits joy, happiness, or fun. When you smile, show a good attitude, a sense of humor, and affection. In the service industry, success requires a smile.

Throughout the day, stop and observe the expression on your face.

O: Open Posture

An open posture shows that your mind is open, while a closed body posture gives the impression that you don't care or don't want to listen. For example, crossing your arms unconsciously creates barriers and prevents positive communication. Think about it the next time you are crossing your arms.

F: Leaning Forward

Leaning forward slightly is a sign that you are attentive and helpful. About two inches is enough, don't lean too much if you fall on top of the other person! The goal here is to unconsciously say, "I'm here for you." Leaning forward clearly conveys this message.

T: Take Notes

The clear, audible, and enthusiastic voice conveys a positive professional message. After swimming for 20 years, I have a coach's voice, and I have scared small animals and children. I accidentally used that sound at the wrong time and made the baby cry. Sometimes I'm walking in an airport and a kid runs down the aisle and without even thinking I shout "Let's go!" I can't help it, too many years on the pool deck.

E: Eye Contact

Eye contact offers valuable social and emotional information, showing that you're paying attention. When you interact with another, you connect with them on a higher level. Once you've done that, get a little comfortable before looking away. You will feel a strong connection.

N: Nod

Nodding shows that you're listening and shows that you don't want to lose the detail of what the other person has to say. I must admit that sometimes I nod to keep my mouth out of trouble. It closes my lips for me, reminding me that it is not yet my turn to speak.

Remember: your reputation is based on the impression you give to each guest or customer. Use SOFTEN technology to enhance conversations with everyone you serve. In our business, positive communication is everything.

SOFTEN contains all the basics for quality body language and is very easy to learn. Keep these principles in mind and put them into action in any situation. It's something that can completely change the tone of the conversation. So when you're in a social situation, remember and use the SOFTEN method.

People can consciously control nonverbal communication over what they say. This is partly because nonverbal communication has more emotion, therefore, more instinctive.

If there is a discrepancy, it is probably based on non-verbal cues instead of the words used.

Inhibiting nonverbal communication can be seen as the speaker carefully regulating their body language and trying to hide their true emotions.

This is a key question because many communication experts believe that nonverbal communication is more effective than words.

Now, I don't think this is always true, but it's true in many major industries, such as initial impressions. If your nonverbal display is not good for you, the other party will quickly have a negative impression of who you are.

The thing is, there are tons of tips on how to use effective body language. It can take years to master because there are so many cues, poses, reactions, and other things to learn. So, the SOFTEN technique plays a very important role in helping people improve their non-verbal communication skills.

In the next chapter I will talk about how to start small talks with other people that work as a trigger for you to start longer and deeper conversations, the prelude to the last chapter, where you will be well prepared to communicate as the best.

Chapter 4: Small Talk as a Fire Starter

After knowing how to use the SOFTEN technique in communications and being sure that at this point you should feel more confident with yourself, applying the different tools that I have been preparing for you, it is time for us to move forward to talk and communicate effectively.

Small talks can be the way for you to stretch the gum and create a good conversation, but let's not go fully, but step by step.

Conversation Starters

Remember when you were a kid? You saw things as a game, and if something made you nervous, you interpreted it as emotion, not fear. You would go to that new neighbor's house and ask if you could come in and say hello and that's it, they became friends, it probably wasn't difficult, just asking if they wanted to play. And they were best friends. Some of the best friendships of my life have been made this way.

What changed that we now isolate ourselves and feel anxious at social events? Well, the passage of time has allowed us to see the bitter face of society. Having been rejected a few times, we learn not to expose ourselves so cheerfully.

According to a study from the University of Chicago, this leads us to falsely believe that strangers don't want to talk to us.

Remember what your mom told you over and over again? "Don't talk to strangers."

But the reality is different. In the same study, a group of volunteers was asked to start a conversation with a stranger on the subway. They predicted that these conversations would cause them anxiety and discomfort, but it turned out that they felt much better talking to a stranger than remaining silent during the trip.

In addition, all participants who tried to talk to someone were successful. None refused.

At the end of the day, we make the mistake of thinking people don't want to talk to us. And since the stranger sitting next to us also believed it, the result was that no one took the first step.

Effective Strategies to Start a Conversation

People expect someone to reveal the magic phrase that would allow them to start a conversation with anyone in any situation.

The problem is that too much weight is given to the prayer itself when in reality it means nothing. Of course, your attitude in saying this is more important, and more importantly, just reaching out and opening your mouth has done more than many people.

For more shy people, some of the following strategies have also proven to be very effective in starting conversations.

Release Shame with the Mask Technique

Although as a child I was quite peaceful, everything changed when a certain time of year arrived: Mardi Gras. That day, I wore denim or samurai clothes, ran, jumped, and played with my friends, a behavior that was completely out of my character.

During my adolescence, I found that this transformation was repeated in the works of the Institute. When I played my character on stage, I dared to face any situation. I still have that feeling to this day every time I have to bring a character to life. You can do the same.

The masking technique consists of creating an alter ego, a character that takes you away from everyday reality so that you can do and say things that you would not normally do. That way, if someone rejects you, you can be sure that they are not rejecting you, but your character.

Actors and comedians like Daniel Tosh use this technique to overcome their shyness on stage. Even Beyoncé created an alter ego named Sasha for her turn to act. In both cases, an outgoing and challenging personality was created and manifested in due time.

Logically, overcoming shyness by facing its roots is much better in the long run, but the masking technique is a very useful tool to start behaving in a more open and sociable way.

Don't Forget the Goal

This is the main reason why many people fail before they even try.

When you want to start a conversation with someone, you should be clear that your goal is not to impress them, try to please them, or seem like an interesting person. People don't know you, and any of these three attempts could easily be interpreted as something against you.

- Your goal should be to simply present yourself as a calm person who wants to have a conversation and see if there are common grounds.

- Later, you can set more specific secondary goals, such as exchanging business cards or calling each other to meet next time, but you shouldn't think about that now.

Once you've made it clear that your goal is to find common interests and translate them into conversations, you won't be distracted by other issues that distract you.

Smile and the World Will Smile at You

Before pronouncing the first word, this simple gesture can make or break a first impression.

By now, we all know the power of a smile, but there are even studies that confirm that when you meet strangers on the street, just nodding your head and smiling can create a bond.

Not to mention all the research that shows that smiling increases your attractiveness.

That's not to say it forces a smile on your face forever. It wouldn't be honest, and it would seem unnatural. Smiling isn't just about your attitude. When you approach someone for the first time to start a conversation, you should do so in a positive and friendly way.

Show that you are here to give energy, not to take it away. Nobody wants to live half an hour with ashes, so first you have to predispose people not to see you as that kind of person. Smile and others will smile back.

Below are some example sentences that may seem strange without the correct intonation and nonverbal language. Therefore, the most important point on this list is undoubtedly this.

Prepare the Ground with a Simple Phrase

"How about your day?" "How are you?" "Hello, how are you doing?"

I could offer more variations, but the goal is for your interlocutor to answer that it is fine. These types of questions are especially interesting because a study showed that by answering "yes," your interlocutor will be more inclined to be social.

When someone tells you they're good or great, they rarely act negatively right away. So it's a good idea to make your first sentence a simple "Hi, how are you?"

- If the person is doing something or just out of politeness, it's also a good idea to start asking permission with "Excuse me" or "Forgive me." Especially when you want to join a group conversation because it demonstrates courtesy and understanding of the other person's social situation.

- Asking if you can interrupt is another good idea, as research shows that trying to be consistent with your answers increases your interlocutor's willingness to talk to you.

Ask Something Related to the Situation or Place

Perhaps the most natural way to start a conversation is to comment or ask a question about a situation that you and the other person have shared. It is not that it is less effective for its simplicity, after all, it is the only link you have before you meet.

This way of starting a conversation also prevents shy people from being rejected in this situation, as they can always show that they just wanted to ask something.

Initial questions don't have to be particularly witty: the best sentences are simple and should only refer to shared circumstances or situations. Ideally, an open-ended question so they can't just answer yes or no. Here are a few examples:

- In a bar: "Excuse me, what time will they close here?"

- In a training course: "In which classroom will they give the talk?"

- At the station: "Do you know if the train to the north has already passed?"

Even if you think a problem may be too obvious, don't worry. These phrases can mean that you need the information, or that you simply want to start a conversation, so it doesn't matter what you say.

Show Curiosity About What They're Doing

This tactic isn't the best if the person isn't doing anything special (like waiting at a bus stop), but it can be useful at a gym, social club, or bar.

Also, you rarely expose yourself, as you just seem to be a curious person. As long as your attitude is positive and not critical, this is a very safe way to start a conversation.

At the gym, you can ask someone who is exercising, for example, "Excuse me, what muscles are you working with this exercise?" On the football field, you can ask the person next to you if they are blowing a vuvuzela, and even in a restaurant, you can ask the customer at the next table what they ordered, with the excuse that it looks good.

Give a Compliment and Continue with a Question

This option is useful when the person you want to talk to doesn't do anything punctual or interesting and the situation doesn't bind you in any way.

It involves starting with a sincere compliment, making the other person nice to you (likes, tastes), and moving on to asking a question to open the conversation.

Some formulas that have given me good results are to value someone's clothes, shoes, or cell phone, for example:

"That tie pairs well with the suit. Where did you buy it?"

"I like your glasses; are they sold in Rome?"

Ask for a Recommendation, Advice, or Opinion

This one is similar to the previous one but with a slight difference. First of all, multiple studies have shown that asking someone's opinion is too positive to make a good first impression. Everyone likes to be valued, and one of the easiest ways to do that is to ask for recommendations.

When you ask someone for their opinion, you are implicitly showing that you value their judgment, which is a compliment. Logically, if you don't know this person, your interest shouldn't be too deep.

- "Excuse me, what model is that phone? I'm thinking about changing mine."

- "Excuse me, I saw that you were reading Murakami's latest book. Would you recommend it?"

- "Hello, if you come here often, would you mind pointing me to a good dish?"

The idea is that you use the situation and background of the person you want to talk to look for references and develop the conversation from there.

Fill in Information Gaps

So far, we have seen very indirect ways to start a conversation, but the best way is explicit sincerity.

Clear honesty is nothing more than filling in information gaps. This is done by answering what, why, and for what. The reason is that many times the information we present is incomplete, which leads our interlocutors to end up filling it with their imagination. This doesn't always work in our favor.

Note the difference:

"Hello, what is your name?"

Here you do not provide any information, your interlocutor can imagine what you want. Maybe you think you want to flirt with him/her, or you recognize him/her but don't remember his/her name, or you want to get his/her attention for some reason. You can't control what your interlocutor thinks of you.

"Hi, I'm trying to meet new people instead of talking to old ones. Do you mind if I show up? Is this how we know each other?"

In this case, you can indicate what you want (introduce yourself), why you want to do it (because you always talk to the same people), and what you want to do (meet new people). You don't allow misunderstandings.

Being honest and clear about what you want is probably the most natural way to start a conversation with a stranger. It takes practice, but once you get the hang of it, the chances of being rejected are very low.

Give a Way Out and Avoid Rejection

Finally, another way to reduce the chances of the other person telling you they're badmouthing right now is to offer them an easy way out.

People usually get defensive when a stranger approaches them because they are not sure if it is going to be extended and fear that they will not be able to get rid of it for long.

To prevent your interlocutor from being invaded by such thoughts, give him the exit yourself. This means that at the beginning of the conversation, you mention that you can only talk for a short time because someone is waiting for you somewhere else. This frees them from feeling tied to you and gives both of you a comfortable outlet if things don't go as expected.

Also, when people think you have to leave as soon as possible, they relax. If you approach someone in a bar and say, "Hi, I want to meet you," their defenses kick in. Who are you? What do you want? So when are you leaving? It was the three questions that bothered him. By filling in the information gaps, you can answer the first two questions, but you should also be able to answer the last question.

"Hi, I'm waiting for some friends and since it looks like you're waiting too, I was wondering if I could sit with you for 5 minutes until they arrive. Do you mind?"

If the conversation goes well, don't worry, no one will remember the 5 minutes you mentioned at the beginning.

Why It Can Fail

With these tools, you will usually succeed, but there is no perfect formula and everyone is going to have a bad day. Unfortunately, many people don't realize that when someone else doesn't accept them, it's often for reasons that have nothing to do with them.

Maybe the other person is having a bad day, maybe you're the tenth person who approaches them and they're exhausted, or maybe they're waiting for someone in a bad mood. The reasons are endless, so trying to understand them is a waste of time.

Once the conversation is started, it can also fail because you simply do not have much in common, or because (this is much more common than you think) your interlocutor is not very good and needs to improve their social skills.

Practice, Practice, and Practice

Conversational skills can be improved. No one is born with them, we all learn them in one way or another, whether from our parents, siblings, or friends.

As learning them later is difficult and because rejection usually affects you more, it is ideal to start practicing in situations where there are no consequences, such as with your hairdresser, taxi driver, or delivery man. These people are there to get paid to take care of you, so it's a good idea to practice a bit in these environments.

There's no better or worse way to start a conversation, and there's certainly no right or wrong line. While you've seen the general concepts in this chapter, the key is, to be honest, and use body language and tone of voice that build intimacy.

Don't aim perfectly to start a conversation, or you'll miss a lot of opportunities. No one expects you to be perfect since your interlocutors also know the effort involved.

You can be funnier, more formal, deeper, or more passionate, but the important thing is who you are. Trying to talk to someone and getting rejected is definitely more successful than sitting in a corner regretting another missed opportunity.

Learn How to Start Deepening the Conversation

Having meaningful conversations with those around us can improve our mood and help us feel more satisfied with our lives. How do you get to that point?

Trivial talk is when the other person doesn't know you as well as before you started the conversation. While it can be tedious to keep talking about the weather or how excited you are for the weekend with someone you barely know, studies have confirmed that these meaningless conversations have many mental health benefits, as they improve mood and strengthen confidence in the goodwill of others. In other words, because of these "little conversations," we tend to see other people with whom we share our lives on a more human and enjoyable level.

But in the end, the most valuable thing is when the dialogue is of special importance for the interlocutor. Those great conversations where you go from the sacred and the human to the personal and intimate where you end up learning more about the person in front of you and seeding the hallucinations for another time. In it, you will find the way.

The quality of a conversation depends on many factors, which we can summarize by exchanging substantive information that concerns us or that directly challenges us. At that point, not only do you learn something more about the person you're talking to, but from them you learn more about who you are, about yourself, and the world you're in. But for this it is necessary to develop a good self-expression, that is, to be honest with anyone who is in front of you.

Self-expression is the number one quality needed to have a good and meaningful conversation. Most of us feel the desire and need to share our thoughts, explore, and inquire about the things that are important to us. So, having the opportunity to crystallize all those abstract thoughts in our heads and share them with the audience for validation helps us feel understood.

In the next chapter, I will delve into this point, because I want to dedicate a wide knowledge of how to establish from a trivial conversation deep conversation and that you know other people, that you connect and empathize with people who change to a deeper conversation.

Chapter 5: Establishing a Deep Connection

In the previous chapter, I told you about the connections you can start making with people, the step for them to talk and make an ephemeral friendship, now, it is time for deep connection, in this chapter, I will teach you how.

Have great conversations that go deeper and meet new people.

It is very important and offers many benefits. It allows you to make a good impression, build strong relationships faster and more efficiently, and create unforgettable memories.

Let's not underestimate the importance of relationships. They are a very important element of our well-being and occupy a large part of our lives! Therefore, invest the necessary time in communicating your interest in technology.

Psychology and understanding relationships are some of my favorite topics, I have worked to get resources to provide the most comprehensive guidance possible.

One of the tricks, whenever you start a conversation with a stranger or someone you don't know very well, is to talk about something that just happened to you that day.

This prevents you from insulting the person as if it were a direct question and allows you to return the question as an answer or increase their knowledge of the subject.

Don't underestimate the number of great conversations you can start by saying "I just had the best pasta I've ever had in Italy!"

Propose a Personal Topic

This may seem obvious when it comes to forming a strong connection with someone, but it's not so obvious when it comes to putting it into practice.

Personal questions are most effective in a relaxed atmosphere with friends we know.

This is the best way to get to know someone better in a deeper way. Personal questions also show that you are interested and want to hear what the other person has to say.

Breaking the Ice: Avoiding Excessively Banal Greetings

From the beginning of the conversation, you can avoid the first "small talk" and get away from the usual greetings. For example, by asking: "What do you do?", you put your interlocutor at a "dead end," he can only tell you about his work.

You can give that question a spin like this:

- What makes you someone different?

- What characterizes you?

This will surely provoke a smile and surprise all our interlocutors.

Formulas in a powerful way and directly touches the essence itself, what makes us who we are, what makes us unique and special. You might even discover something a little crazy that no one else knows: who knows, maybe he's a doctor by day and a rock star by night?

If you've seen the person before but they don't have a friendship yet, you can try to break the ice with a simple question like "How was your weekend? What's new?"

But often the answer is vague, with few details.

That's why I suggest you better ask yourself: "What was the best thing about your weekend?" or "Do you want to do something special this week?"

In this way, the person can tell you a story that allows you to know more about him and his motivations.

These tips also apply when you're asked what you do (among other things): instead of just saying you're a student or Erasmus, you can encourage conversation by adding details of things you've done that relate to yours or your accommodation.

Also, if you're asked what you're doing to have fun or take a break, talk about a recent time when you've enjoyed your hobby, whether it's attending a piano concert or jogging in the park.

Raise Questions About Your Life and Experiences

Another effective way to address personal issues without being too intrusive is to ask about the other person's experiences. It's best to approach positive experiences because according to psychology, other people will associate those positive experiences with you and keep you in a good place.

To make this more concrete, here are some examples:

- How did you feel living in another city and coming here?

- How was your trip to Madrid for that project?

- How did you know you wanted to teach German in Berlin?

- What was the hardest hurdle you had to overcome?

Try to Establish a True Relationship

There is no need to force a conversation. Try to talk about things that the other person is passionate about and that you are also interested in. That way, the relationship is real, and that person will be more willing to talk about it in depth.

Another psychological factor to consider is not assuming that the other person is bored or uninterested in the conversation. Because, in that way, it unintentionally influences the discussion and undermines it.

On the other hand, imagine that the other person is also interested in having a deep conversation and that they have a lot to teach you.

Discover Your Goals and Dreams

Asking someone about their goals is one way to understand how they hope to progress. Knowing a person's goals and dreams can encourage them to open up to you and talk about their innermost ones, ensuring discussions are lively and interesting.

They can be targets from different fields (professional concerns, fitness, lifestyle, hobbies, etc...)

Here are some concrete examples:

- What would you like to be in life?

- What goals do you want to achieve over the next 3 years?

Take an Interest in Your Family

Families shape people in important ways and affect them throughout their lives. Knowing about someone's family can bring many things. You can start with basic questions and move on to more important aspects.

For example, ask "How many siblings do you have?" followed by "Do you get along with your family?" or "What's your relationship?"

But keep in mind that not everyone likes to talk about their family. Be respectful if the person seems upset or changes the subject.

Ask Questions About Your Profession Instead of Your Job

From a professional point of view, it is preferable to ask questions about someone's career, and can be a good way to approach them. For those who feel stuck at work, talking about their studies and their expectations can go a long way in encouraging them to realize they have other options.

For example, if you want to talk to a coworker, ask them what brought them here or what they like best. You can also ask where they want to go or what their career goals are.

On the contrary, if your interlocutor does not like his work very much, I recommend that you avoid this topic. You might try asking him some questions about his hobbies. Often, you can learn more about a person by asking about their hobbies instead of their job.

So even if you're doing the same thing, try to keep the person more personal and away from professional problems.

Remember Your Previous Conversations

One way to show respect for this person is to remember previous conversations and what was important to them.

For example, if you know you've just returned from a trip, are about to travel the world, or have just moved to Italy, ask him. This will show that you listen to him and that you care about his life.

This can also help you get to know her better and open the door to more conversations.

Here is a concrete example:

"How did the exam go for you? I see that you have worked hard."

Another benefit of recovering an old theme is that it evokes a feeling of nostalgia.

Acknowledging past events and remembering them is a surefire way to generate gratitude. According to a psychology study by "Clay Routledge," commenting on moments shared by two people can increase feelings of social connection and make them more respected.

To delve into nostalgia, I suggest talking about your upbringing, childhood, and adolescence. This allows you to form an intimate connection with others. By expressing everything you felt in your youth or what you did wrong as a child, you allow the other person to understand what shaped you as an adult.

Ask Open-Ended Questions

A conversation is not talking to someone: it is the conversation itself that must affect the person. By asking open-ended and interesting questions, you'll learn more about each other's perspectives and experiences. If the person is telling you something, go ahead and ask them a question that encourages them to continue the conversation.

The idea is to keep the question open so that others can continue as they wish. It's hard to have deep conversations with yes or no answers because we're at a dead end.

This can also be more informative, giving the other person a chance to explore and share their thoughts and opinions.

For example, instead of asking someone else: Do you like living in Rome? you could ask: How do you feel living here?

Or even ask other questions:

- What do you think of this?

- What would you like to go and do?

- What do you think of this?

Follow Up with Deeper Questions

Instead of flipping through a few different topics, don't hesitate to ask for more information about the answers above and help the other person open up.

In short, if you ask a general question, ask a more specific one. Your questions should engage the other person and help create depth in the conversation.

For example, if someone brings up a souvenir of a trip, you can immediately ask: "How did this trip change your life?" or "What did you take away from this experience?"

But be careful not to ask questions one after another, this is not to turn the discussion into an interrogation or give the impression of a police interrogation!

Ask good questions that show your commitment.

One of the best ways to show engagement is to show a natural curiosity about what the other person has to say.

Make sure you ask at least one question before moving on to the next topic. Gathering details can increase your chances of connecting with others. This stage can also find a way to reach out and help others (but I'll talk about that later).

Similarly, spend less time talking about yourself.

People spend about 60% of their time talking, talking about themselves, which causes the brain to release dopamine and we feel good. But deep conversations require a balanced back-and-forth exchange between two people. So, remember the change in time and balance.

Find Common Interests and Experiences

A simple and easy way to connect with someone is to find common interests, hobbies, and experiences with the person you're talking to. Maybe they grew up together, went to the same university, or watched the same TV shows. Ask what their route is, and if yours is similar, compare!

Because it's no coincidence that dating sites bring people together based on what they have in common: Several studies have shown that shared interests keep relationships strong.

When two people share common interests, there are fewer disagreements and problems between them.

For example, if the person is sad because something happened to them in the office and you have had a similar experience, you both realize how difficult it is to make changes in everyday life. Telling stories about difficult relationships often brings meaning and comfort.

Even if you don't have a similar experience, you can show that you understand and listen.

For example, you can say something like: I don't understand any of that, but I'm fascinated by people who work in that area, you must have worked hard!

When you're looking for common ground, don't expect deep themes to immediately come to mind. If you have no inspiration, one trick is to talk about psychology or any other topic that has to do with how we behave. Because in this realm, we are all in this together: we interact with other people, and we act together with others.

Another excellent source of interesting ideas about the world and about ourselves are the "TED" talks. They are congresses whose motto "ideas worth sharing" explains the concept well. You can easily find these videos on "YouTube" or on their website. I guarantee you'll find a theme that inspires you. The advantage is that it gives you easy, very interesting, and deep topics to share in discussions.

Discover the Preferences of Others

Knowing what those people like or dislike allows us to better understand what they have in mind. It seems to be self-explanatory, but most of us forget to ask about other people's tastes.

Like asking them what activities they enjoy the most, or what they appreciate most in their relationships with others... Knowing their perspective can only help us be better interlocutors and improve communication.

Also, learning to comfort each other during difficult times is a very important asset.

Ask "How can I help you?" or "How would you like me to behave when you're depressed/hurting?" Guaranteed to build intimacy and strengthen friendly relationships.

Also, pay attention to the person's body language and its potential meaning.

Try to pay attention to a person's mouth movements and tone of voice when developing a conversation, and try to detect what they like.

Stay Ready to Be Vulnerable

It can be difficult to maintain and build a deep dialogue if those involved do not want to be vulnerable. Being vulnerable means letting others know that you can't always be fair, strong, or perfect. Share your imperfections in a way that doesn't elicit sympathy, but shows that you're aware of the difficulties.

Another way to be vulnerable is to share experiences, and personal memories, and hold the other person accountable. Be prepared to open up, especially if you feel lonely in front of something.

But take some precautions: if someone shows you vulnerability, make sure you don't judge or criticize them based on their experiences. Try saying something like, "You've shown great willpower to overcome this obstacle."

In other words, to form a unique relationship, you must be willing to reveal a few things about yourself and talk about your feelings and learnings. It is not necessary to reveal big secrets or anything like that, just something personal.

Revealing something about oneself predisposes others to do the same.

Give and Ask for Advice

I admit that this technique may require a lot of guts for some, but it works very well.

Research shows that seeking advice can also help you appear more competent and turn the other person into an ally.

Offering advice becomes one of the strongest forms of engagement between two people. From the moment you inform your loved one about the challenges you are facing, it means you are ready, to be honest with them and care about them.

These two signals combine to convey a high level of confidence and create a deeper sense of intimacy. Because of the trust between two people, in the end, there will be results.

Asking for advice, on the other hand, refers to the previous point: encouraging him to express his vulnerability and also promoting intimacy.

But be careful not to abuse unsolicited advice! It is necessary to put the person in front of you and check his reaction.

Giving advice that others have not asked for triggers a defensive attitude (maximizing our freedom and our decision-making based on human needs).

If you have doubts about how the other person will respond to your proposal, it is best to ask the question head-on and express empathy for their situation, for example: "This seems difficult, have you thought about what you are going to do?

Show That You Care About the Other

Deep conversations don't have to be long conversations or exhaustive conversations. Show that you care about the other person, that you support them, and that you want to help them.

Small gestures can mean a lot, so celebrate the other person's success and show them that you're here to talk, especially if they're going through a tough time.

For example, share your enthusiasm when you find out that she won a scholarship, passed her exams, and was accepted on the Erasmus trip... Offer your support and help in a meaningful way, whether it's through a text message, email, or face-to-face. conversation.

Consider How You Can Add Value to the Conversation

It's important to ask yourself how you can add value to someone through a conversation. It can include information, thoughts, advice... In a word, useful things that people don't know but that work for them. When you truly understand someone's priorities, you'll be surprised at the number of opportunities to connect with them.

On the other hand, one study showed that happier people avoid superficial trivia conversations and engage in deep conversations twice as often as less happy people.

What you need to remember is to value other people's time and use it wisely: value the time spent talking, skip trivial conversations, and figure out how you and that person can help each other.

Do What Can Help You

People will appreciate the relationship more if you stick to your suggestion: a contact, something useful, a specific piece of information, or a fact.

Remember, dopamine is released when we talk about ourselves and our experiences. Well, when you share something with someone (whether it's a deep secret, a dream, or an aspiration), our pleasure centers also turn on and another hormone called oxytocin is released. Another name for oxytocin? The hormone of love because it plays a very important role in creating a bond between two people.

According to my research, studies show that the release of oxytocin makes us more sympathetic, understanding, and open to our feelings. The release of oxytocin will help manage conflicts more effectively and reduce social stress hormones.

Listen Instead of Planning Your Response

Focusing on the words of the interlocutor activates neurons in the brain and helps it retain information (rather than planning and panicking about your next reaction), according to a study.

So, try to ignore the thoughts that come to you and pay your full attention to what you say. If you must do this (which I strongly recommend), take a moment to review your answers before it's your turn to start talking.

In ancient China it was believed that everyone had a "monkey spirit" that jumped from one thought to another: "What would he/she think of me? Am I making a good impression? I must get to the train station."

This constant mental noise not only distracts them from each other and the conversation, but also from their perspective, priorities, and goals.

If you listen to your "monkey spirit," you will only understand a small part of what the other person is saying. Therefore, you will misunderstand everything, you will remember badly what was said.

So don't get too excited about your next idea. People may notice when you're not listening because you can't wait to share your next thought. Before they finish, he is already eager to tell them about the amazing experience he just had or participate in it right away.

Try to listen before you speak. If your story is funny, it will still be funny five minutes later. Even if you forget what you were trying to say, you will eventually remember it when the context arises.

So it's about practicing active listening. Instead of thinking about how you should interact, take the time to listen and try to understand what that person is saying when they speak.

Pay attention to what he says, how he feels, and the messages he conveys through his body language. If you don't understand what was said or want to respond directly to something, ask if you misunderstood so they can repeat it to you.

Sometimes being an active listener can force us to be quiet too. Showing that you're comfortable with silence, even an "awkward silence," gives the other person time to mentally rephrase and find the right words without feeling abrupt.

Recognize What You Just Heard

After the other party has finished speaking, talk again and repeat what you just said in summary. This confirms that you are listening to the other person, not to yourself ("monkey spirit").

This also prevents you from continuing the conversation in case of misunderstanding. Give the other person a chance to correct you or further expand their thinking to make sure you understand them.

Value their experiences and people feel heard and understood: show that you are listening to them. When you give someone value, you show them that you accept them and that what they say matters.

Assessments can be as simple as "This seems so difficult!" or "No wonder it's been so difficult and stressful!" Assessments create connection and a sense of security, which is important in deep conversations.

Don't forget that if you see every conversation as an opportunity to get others to embrace your values and beliefs, you'll have a hard time getting them to stay. After all, no one wants to be a missionary.

As concrete examples, you could explain using statements like "So you mean..." or "It's funny that you feel that way because..." or "That's a point worth thinking about..."

Displays Open Body Language

Your body can communicate to the other person that you are listening and engaged. Nod, smile, and use facial expressions to show your concern from time to time. Check your posture to make sure it's open and comfortable for the other person.

What I mean by that is that it's best not to look at the person with arms and legs crossed when they are speaking in a relaxed posture and with benevolent eye contact.

But most importantly, avoid forcing exaggerated and open body language, as it's easy for people to realize it's "fake" and have the opposite effect.

Address the Conversation Openly

This point has to do with dialogue, where you don't necessarily share the same perspective as the other person. My advice is not to stray from different topics or perspectives, as this makes the discussion richer and more interesting.

If you disagree with something, listen to the other person and consider their point of view. Instead of pretending to win the conversation or pretend you're right, set a goal to better understand the other person and get a different perspective.

For example, if you're used to discussing politics with your best friend, try to deepen the conversation by listening carefully to the other person and being willing to consider their point of view.

Identify Each Person and Integrate Them into the Conversation

If you are arguing with several people or if someone is nearby, be sure to include "foreigners" in the conversation.

Too often, people focus on talking to just one person and forget to include someone who can make a difference and bring a lot of richness to the conversation.

Copy the Good Speakers

One of my favorite tips is to watch the actors on stage and listen to talk show hosts and other normal people you think are attractive.

Try to remember the types of questions they ask, the way they respond to others, and even their silence and body language.

They'll probably learn the same way: by observing, taking notes, and (most importantly) doing.

Sincerity

After all, it's easy to say, "You know, I'm not wasting time talking about rain and good weather, why don't we talk about something deeper?

Your interlocutor may be surprised at first, but then feel relieved to know that you have rights and that you do not deserve to talk about small things.

I recommend that you always have some "deep" questions ready to foster intimacy, especially: "What are you afraid of today?" and "Are you happy with the way you live now?"

Admit Some of Your Past Failures

Usually, if you talk about your accomplishments, chances are they'll just shake their heads and say, "Congratulations, that's great!" That doesn't provide many conversations.

However, since you reported an accident or failure, others are more likely to react and start talking about their mishaps. It also allows you to communicate life lessons and help others not make the same mistakes as you.

For example, you can talk about the time you accidentally spilled food on other people in a restaurant or accidentally burned a homemade pizza you wanted to take to a party, or even when you accidentally dropped your phone in a public container and were caught trying to get it.

These are just examples to give you an idea of what I'm talking about! It's up to you to modify them and choose the (best) ones that will make others laugh.

Don't Multitask While Talking to Someone

A small note, but one that seems important to me, is when one person is talking and the other is on the phone.

The brain has difficulty concentrating on sounds and images at the same time, according to a study. Get away from your phone/tablet/tv/book (and any other activity) and focus your full attention on the conversation and come back to it later.

Develop the Conversation Patiently

One study explains that online communication can create a false sense that just a few lines of dialogue can create the illusion of a passionate and engaged conversation.

But if you're face-to-face, don't feel bad if you don't have a deep conversation right away! Continue to develop communication and listening skills and actively connect with others.

Show Gratitude to the Other

Numerous psychological studies have shown that gratitude is good for our body, mind, and relationships.

Whether it's expressing appreciation or expressing appreciation for someone else's good works, gratitude strengthens our relationships.

Gratitude has many consequences: it builds trust and intimacy, brings greater satisfaction to our relationship, and encourages you and the person you're arguing with to go further in their relationship (regardless of whether you're still meeting or forging friendships).

When you get that person's approval to do something, it creates great reciprocity and motivates the other person to come back.

Through this chain reaction, each of you will feel more grateful for the other, which will strengthen your relationship. How amazing it is!

Conclusion

So, instead of going for the classic questions:

- What do you do?

- How is your work going?

- How are you doing at school?

- Have you been able to catch up on yesterday's homework?

- What's new?

- How is your sister?

Try deeper questions:

- What fills you the most with life?

- If you could study something else again, what would it be?

- What was your favorite book as a child?

- Do you like your name? Have you had the desire to change it?

- Do you have someone to inspire you as a mentor?

- Why do you currently recognize yourself?

- If it didn't depend on money, what would you like to do for free?

- Is there anything you would like to overcome?

- What is an ideal day for you?

- Tell me a word to describe you.

- What happened that day you were proud of yourself?

- What do you lack in life?

- What dreams do you have to fulfill?

- What fills you with the most excitement right now?

- Have you changed much these 5 years?

- What are the best and worst moments of your childhood?

- What would you do with your money if you were the richest in the world?

- What would you like to achieve in the coming years?

I could go on a lot more, because by combining all the techniques mentioned above, you can generate countless questions that will lead to deep, rich, and interesting conversations, and most importantly, that will strengthen your relationships with others.

Another great exercise is to ask yourself questions, you are sure to learn a lot!

Even if these questions seem strange in the middle of a banal conversation (because let's face it, we don't get these questions every day), arm yourself with courage!

Indeed, your interlocutor will be surprised, but if you feel that he has opened up to you, I guarantee the result.

Now, you know what you have to do to make the most of the new knowledge and friends you will make facing that shyness and introversion.

As a final point, in the process when you talk to the person use:

- Body language similar to that of the person, without it being a crude imitation.

- Find yourself to tell something and then invite the person to say it too, like a two-way game of tennis.

- Ask meaningful questions that don't answer yes or no and that prompt you to tell things.

- Smile and reflect gentle body language.

- Do not speak accelerated as if you were out of the air in it, quiet, and enjoy the road.

The practice will help that over time you get to talk well with others, making deep connections and friendships, that they know that you are an interesting conversationalist, and as a final point, stay updated, look for topics to talk about, because if you have nothing in your mind to say, then all this path we have traveled will be of little use.

Printed in Great Britain
by Amazon